OVERWHELMED BY MY BLESSINGS

30 DAYS OF ENCOURAGEMENT FOR MOMS

Volume 1

ROBIN MEADOWS

Cover and graphic design: Abbi Meadows

Photography: Riley Klaassen

For moms everywhere.
You are the bravest.

CONTENTS

Acknowledgements / 7
Introduction / 9

1. YOU ARE THE MOM / 13

2. SET THE TONE / 16

3. TOO MUCH/ 19

4. EMBRACE / 22

5. GIVE/ 25

6. PSALMS 102 / 28

7. PUT IT IN THE BASKET / 31

8. OVERWHELMED / 34

9. CHOOSE YOUR THOUGHTS / 37

10. EMOTIONS / 40

11. DREAD / 43

12. MIRRORS OR LIGHTS? / 46

13. JUST SMILE / 50

14. WORDS ARE ETERNAL / 53

15. THERMOSTAT / 56

16. OPPORTUNITIES? / 59

17. YOU AREN'T ENOUGH / 62

18. PRESSURE / 65

19. PRESSED / 68

20. MODEL IT / 71

21. DARK THOUGHTS / 75

22. ENCOURAGE YOURSELF / 79

23. ENCOURAGING WOMEN / 82

24. ENCOURAGE YOUR CHILDREN / 86

25. ENCOURAGING MEN / 90

26. INTERRUPTIONS / 95

27. VISION CORRECTION / 98

28. MOM GUILT / 101

29. WHO IS IN CHARGE? /105

30. UNIQUE / 109

ACKNOWLEDGEMENTS

Thank you to the great team at YouVersion.
Without you, this series may never have been an idea.

To my friend and editor, Amanda Lounder—your
countless hours of editing make me better.

To my lovely daughter-in-law, Abbi Meadows—your
editing, graphic and artistic skills continually impress
me, as do you.

To my amazing children—all of you. You are my
blessings and have taught me more than you will ever
know. I love you each with a passion that cannot be
explained unless you are a mother.

To my tribe—you know me and love me anyway. You
sharpen me.

To Jesus—my hope. You are my life, my joy, my all,
and more than enough.

And especially to my God-given, wonderful husband,
Dirk. God knew how much I needed you. These
stories mostly come from the things you taught me.
Thank you for sticking with me for almost 50 years!

INTRODUCTION

I'm a mom. While I always wanted to be a mom, I certainly never planned to have seven children (four girls, three boys), move to the country, and home-educate all of them! But, in following my husband and the direction of God, I did. We launched all those kids and lived to tell about it. The great news is they lived through it too! It wasn't easy. Often, it wasn't fun for them or for me, and I was ready to run away.

I believed my children were gifts from God, but I was very overwhelmed by these blessings. Through the 35 years of raising our seven, my heart was radically changed. It was a long, difficult process, with many tears and much wrestling with God. This journey of motherhood changed me in the best of ways.

I also never planned to write about these experiences in a book or devotional series. But I did, and I am. That's the beauty of a relationship with Jesus: He takes our past experiences and our current place in life and turns them into His purpose. That's what He did for me. That's what He is doing with you, no matter the season you are in.

This compilation includes the first six installments of my devotional plan entitled "Overwhelmed by My Blessings: Encouragement for Moms" which was originally featured on the YouVersion Bible app (www.bible.com). This book came about thanks to the many requests moms were sending me after reading the series online. This version has been expanded to include reflection questions which can be explored individually or in a group setting.

It is my hope and prayer that in reading these devotionals and looking up the scriptures, you will be encouraged that with a strong, committed, daily relationship with our loving Father, your hope will grow and your faith will stand firm. Moms need that to be healthy: mind, soul, and body.

Purchase a pretty notebook or journal to use along with your Bible through the reflection questions at the end of each day's devotional. Take your time, but stay after it. Write out the scriptures that speak to your heart and be honest with your answers to the questions. Consider gathering with some of your mom friends for a group discussion, even if you can only "meet" online!

I pray that the Spirit meets you in your place, allowing my experiences to give you hope and point you to Jesus, your strength for this beautifully broken journey of motherhood. The days may feel long, but the years are short. Hold on to Him!

~Robin

1

YOU ARE A MOM

I know you. You love your kids, but you are beyond tired, past exhaustion, drowning in diapers, laundry, and dirty dishes, and have no idea what you will fix for dinner tonight. On top of that, you are supposed to teach your kids something, or come home from work with a good attitude? It's too much.

All you want is to take a shower without someone screaming outside the bathroom door, and you would give up almost anything for a decent night's sleep. You feel unnoticed, unappreciated, and overwhelmed. You are a mom.

I'm a mom too, although I'm ahead of you on the road. I'm now a 63-year-old proud grandmother of 19 who raised and home educated seven children—who amazingly still like me—and we all lived to tell about it!

I've been where you are. It's hard. Motherhood is no glamorous job, but it's the highest calling you will ever have—a calling that will teach you things you didn't know you needed to know.

This job will eventually end, leaving you with gray hairs, countless wrinkles, saggy skin, and yet, a heart that has grown and expanded in ways you didn't know were possible. If you allow it, this job of motherhood will make you more like Jesus.

Let's be honest—kids are needy. Our constant investment into their lives leaves us feeling depleted and needy, too. That's okay because we are also children. Children of God. He loves us like we love our own children, despite our messiness, our sassy attitudes, and even when we break His heart. He loves us even more than we love our own children. He loves us because we are His.

Just as our children depend on our guidance, He assures us that we don't have to do this mom thing alone. He is with us every step if only we will reach out and ask for His help.

I'm reminded of the story of a little boy, impatiently standing in a long grocery check-out line. His mama holds his small hand firmly as he continually tries to leave her side. "Mama! You are hurting me," he whines loudly.

"I am not the one pulling away, " she answers him.

Weary mama, have you spent time with Him recently? Held His hand? Asked for help?

Father, as Your daughter, Your little girl, I sit at Your feet, weary, worn, and exhausted. I ask for Your strength to be mine. I need You, deeply. May Your great love for me spill over into my love for my children. Today, I choose to stand by Your side, holding Your hand as we face this day together.

Consider reading these passages from The Message:

- Matthew 11:28-30
- Psalms 23:4-5
- John 15:5-8

Take the time to use a notebook or journal to actually write answers to these questions. This process will enable you to dig deep into your thoughts and motives allowing the Spirit of God to minister to your mind and heart.

What things prevent you from spending regular time with Jesus? List them.

What changes will you make to ensure time with Him happens daily?

Do you believe it will be time well spent? Explain.

Do you really believe He is your help? How do your everyday actions show the truth that He is your help?

2

SET THE TONE

When I discovered I was pregnant with our sixth child, I knew I was in way over my head. I was already overwhelmed by my responsibilities, but this put me on the proverbial ledge. I'm a pretty resourceful, determined girl, but this was way more than I could possibly handle. I was homeschooling my four older children while trying to keep an active 3-year-old occupied, and now I had a baby. I tried to have some order to our day and still find a drop of time alone with my husband. I just hoped my kids wouldn't leave home at 18 still unable to read or subtract and that my husband would still love me.

Often, I would walk to our mailbox at the end of our long driveway, look longingly down the road, and seriously wonder what it would be like to just keep walking.

One day, while daydreaming about running away, I heard the gentle whisper of Jesus saying, "Spend some time with Me." What?! I can't even go to the bathroom alone, and the noise level in our house is deafening! Time? I don't have time!

But, I knew I had the same 24-hour days as everyone else. I just had to make time with Jesus a priority. So I began getting up at 5:00 am every day because that was the only time my house was quiet. I started reading my Bible in those early, peaceful hours. At first, I didn't feel like I was receiving much, but after some time those words became peace in the chaos of my day and gave me the power to persevere. God's Word was like chemotherapy for the dark sin in my heart and sight for my blind eyes. Those words became breath, and love, and LIFE! They changed me then and are still changing me today.

Sure, there were days some of my children got out of bed and wanted to join me. I taught them to sit quietly with me or they would have to go back to bed. One of my adult daughters says sitting with me while I read my Bible is still one of her favorite memories.

Try it! I challenge you. Set your alarm 30 minutes earlier. Get up before your household awakens. I promise, time with God will set the tone for your day and set your heart on the right things. You'll see.

Father, I admit I value my sleep. This is a hard one for me, to consider getting up earlier each day. Give me the courage to fight the excuses and choose to honor You with the first part of my day. I ask that as I make this sacrifice of sleep, I will be alert and open to Your words for me. Thank You for Your gentle reminders that Your words are life.

Consider reading these scriptures from The Message for a fresh perspective:

- Hebrews 4:12 -13
- 2 Timothy 3:14-17
- Deuteronomy 11:18-21
- Deuteronomy 32:44-47
- Psalms 119:33-48

Counting backward from the time you have to begin getting ready for work, or from the time your kids awaken, what time would you have to get up to have 30 minutes alone to read your Bible and pray?

Do you believe that His words are life and breath? Using your journal, explain.

What value is there in making daily time with Jesus a practice in your life?

How I delight in your commands!

Psalms 119:47

3

TOO MUCH

I remember one day when my children were young, my husband came home from work and found us all sitting in the floor, crying. **Even me!** I was done. Done in, over-done, and undone. I was looking for the place where mothers go to resign.

"I can't do this anymore," barely getting the words out to my husband through my sobs. "It's too much! They don't listen to me, the house is always a mess. I don't even have time to do the things that **have** to be done just to keep us from living in squalor!"

After settling us all down he later talked to me about a concept I've since used again and again. My gentle man said, "Robin, it's not going to get any easier for quite a while. You're going to have to decide to accept that and do the best you can." Wow! My attitude needed changing.

With a lot of grumbling and struggling, I began to allow those words to go deep into my heart. I began to see things differently. I started making the choice to accept that my days were going to be boring, mundane and uneventful—unless I made them more fun. **I needed to enjoy, rather than escape.**

I was always going to be stressed and overwhelmed unless I learned to accept the fact that with all God had given me, He would also provide a way for me to deal with it in a loving, patient manner.

As I learned to give up my preconceived ideas of how life was supposed to be and give of myself to my children, life got easier. OK…it really didn't. But I was stepping into a new area of personal growth and maturity that benefited me and my family.

Father, please give me the courage to step into the reality that my day is what I make it, based on my attitudes. I invite You into my circumstances. Help me to see with Your eyes, knowing that all I do and say today counts for eternity, and is not wasted effort. I pray for Your strength to be mine, choosing to find joy, —Your abundant joy—even in the most mundane tasks. I place my day in Your hands, agreeing that today is a good day to have a good day!

Scripture readings:

- Isaiah 43:19
- 2 Corinthians 5:17
- Ephesians 4:20-24
- Luke 6:38
- Psalms 118:24
- Nehemiah 8:10

What is the "it" or fear in your life that completely overwhelms you? List one or more in your journal.

Did you, or do you, have expectations that do not

match your present circumstances? Explain.

Realizing your situation may not change any time soon, are there any practical things you can do to help alleviate the pressure you feel? Spend some time praying over this. ("Running away" is not permitted on this list).

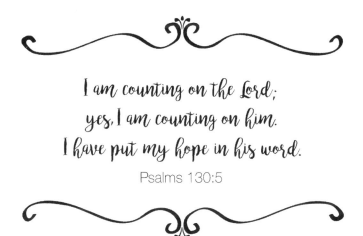

I am counting on the Lord;
yes, I am counting on him.
I have put my hope in his word.

Psalms 130:5

4

EMBRACE

Embracing our situations and circumstances is not a one-time event. Life throws us curves each day, sometimes before breakfast! How in the world do we accept what we are given?

My grace is enough; it's all you need. My strength comes into its own in your weakness. 2 Corinthians. 12:9 –The Message

His grace is enough? It sounds like a religious cliche or a patronizing platitude to our weary ears. But, it is truth and power for us if we'll receive it. (Paul knew; read his account in the surrounding scriptures). God's grace *is* enough for every difficult situation we will ever go through, even if it doesn't seem possible.

We all have a choice. We can buck and fight against our situations, or we can choose to embrace what God has given us. Here's the key: we don't receive His grace until we humble ourselves and admit that we can't do *it* on our own, no matter what our "it" is.

Maybe your difficult circumstances are in dealing with a challenging child or even choosing to love your husband when he's not so lovable. It may be your financial situation, your job, your boss, your singleness, or dealing with parents. Whatever "it" is, when we stop seeing our circumstances as obstacles to defeat or overcome, and choose to step into them, that is the moment when we receive His grace. It means choosing to let go, and allowing Him to be in control. And that is sometimes a hard choice to make.

Striving and bucking against our hard circumstances will eventually defeat us. But, willingly accepting and stepping into the difficulties can do a mighty work in our hearts. His grace is there for this moment—as well as the next.

Embrace to receive His grace!

Oh, Father, this sounds too hard. I am struggling under the burden You have given me, and things are way harder than I ever dreamed possible. I want to accept what You have given me, but I will admit, I want things to be easier than this. Here's what I do know: I can't do this on my own. I need Your supernatural strength and power just to get through today. I repent of trying to figure it out and doing things on my own and I ask You to show Yourself even in the circumstances of my day. I choose to embrace my situation with a new perspective. Please show me Your grace!

Scripture readings:

- James 4:6
- Colossians 1:10-12
- Ephesians 2:8-9
- 2 Peter 1:2
- John 1:16
- Hebrews 4:16

From the list of "its" you made yesterday, what do you most need to embrace?

In what ways might you be bucking and fighting against these difficult people or situations?

In what ways might your peace, health, and relationships improve if you are able to let go and embrace these people and situations through the strength and grace of Jesus? Take some time to write your thoughts down.

But I will keep on hoping for your help;
I will praise you more and more.

Psalms 71:14

5

GIVE

His grace is enough. What does that mean and how in the world do we go about receiving it? We know we first received His grace when we repented of our sins and allowed Him into our hearts. But, why is life so difficult even though we are trying to do the right things? Maybe it's because we aren't receiving that grace each day.

It's really hard to give something you don't have, and grace is no exception. Moms, we are the worst at holding ourselves to such rigid expectations. But, what if it's not about what we *do*, but who we are? We are so tired from doing, that we don't even know how to just "be." Be His.

We need some grace. And His grace is ours for the accepting! I think we've all been taught to believe that we cannot give out unless we are first filled, and that's a problem for overwhelmed wives and moms. Our tanks are empty, and we feel like we are dishing out emotional leftovers.

While I understand the concept of being healthy so we can care for others, I think we often forget about the abundant, overflowing power of the Holy Spirit that is ours. He never runs out, so why do we?

We need to make a mind and heart shift. Let's no longer consider ourselves as vessels for filling so we can then flow onto others. No. We are open-ended conduits of our Father's grace, love, kindness, and power! He constantly gives and gives. As we stay connected to His power and grace, we will remain steadfast in our ability to give and give again. Over and over. Our bodies will be tired, but our spirits can stay renewed.

Tired mama: are you connected? Are you receiving His grace in your life? He is there, waiting for you to turn to Him and accept His lavish life-giving power in your life right now.

*Father, I admit that I have mistakenly thought I had to be filled to the brim with Your presence in my life before I could spill Your love and life onto others, especially my husband and children. I want to stay connected to You, to abide in Your love and grace, knowing that there is nothing I have to **do** but simply **be** open to Your Presence in my heart. I pray that by Your Spirit's power, Your love and grace will flow through me to all I see and speak to today, tomorrow, and all my days. I choose You!*

Consider reading these scriptures from The Message:

- Colossians 1:10-12
- 2 Corinthians 9:8-11
- John 15:1-8
- Galatians 5:22-23

Using your journal, tell how this concept of "being" rather than "doing" speaks to you.

Are you generally hard on yourself? What might be the result to those around you if you were able to find some freedom by offering yourself more grace?

Is it a mind-shift to consider that you don't have to be filled in order to give? That you don't give out from the overflow but from the continual flow of the Holy Spirit? Explain how this change in perspective might make a difference in your mind and heart.

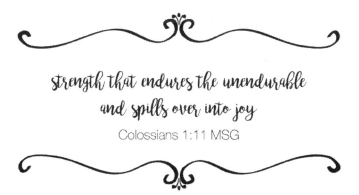

strength that endures the unendurable
and spills over into joy

Colossians 1:11 MSG

6

PSALMS 102

Psalms 102 (NIV) offers such a great, almost humorous picture of us moms on our worst days. Take a minute to read it in your Bible

"My days vanish like smoke." Yes, they either fly by with nothing accomplished or they drag along and bedtime can't come soon enough.

"My heart is blighted and withered like grass." The words my child just yelled at me went deep and hurt worse than they should.

"I forget to eat my food." That's because when you went to the microwave to warm your now-cold lunch, you found your morning coffee.

"I am like a desert owl, [....] like a bird alone on a roof." How in the world can I feel so lonely in a house full of people?

"All day long my enemies taunt me; those who rail against me use my name as a curse." When did I begin seeing my own children as enemies? Why does the word "Mom" so often seem like a curse word?

I remember those days. I even remember saying, "Don't 'mom' me!" Now, a few years later, I can read this and smile, but there were many days when it felt too true. My kids felt like the enemy.

Though our kids are not the enemy, we do have a very real adversary. Satan is out to steal our peace and joy, kill our influence, and destroy our faith. Ultimately, his goal is to take us completely out of our role as loving wife and mother. Be alert to his tactics.

Psalms 102 takes a turn when verse 12 begins with *"But you, Lord."* Let this be our heart's cry. He is faithful and has compassion. He responds to our destitute prayers and yearnings, all for the sake of a future generation. He remains the same; His years will never end.

The chapter ends with this promise: *"The children of your servants will live in your presence; their descendants will be established before you."*

Our children are not our enemies. They are our future, and God's legacy of love.

Father, thank You that we can even find humor in Your Word. Today, I ask for a lightness in my spirit and to remember that my children are not the enemy, but my legacy. Help me be mindful and alert to the real enemy who is out to kill, steal, and destroy, knowing that when I call on You, he has to leave.

Read these scriptures in a few different versions:

- Psalms 102
- John 10:10
- James 1:12

Do you read God's Word as if He is speaking to you personally? Explain.

Do you approach your children as if they are the enemy, rather than knowing that you have a very real enemy? Be honest. Are you alert to the enemy's tactics, or do you need to become more aware?

What personal triggers does the enemy use to steal your peace and joy? List them.

In your journal, write your hope of the Godly influence you will have on your children and your husband in the years to come.

But you, Lord

Psalms 102:12

7

PUT IT IN THE BASKET

What is consuming your mind this morning? What is it that has you distracted and is keeping you from focusing on these words? What thoughts are rising up, making you believe your worst fears will happen?

What if I tell you there is a way to let those thoughts, stresses, and fears go?

Look up Exodus 2:1-10. Try The Message version for a quick, easy read.

You'll notice this mom also had a dilemma. Her problem isn't the same as yours, but I'm sure it consumed her every thought. She was trying to protect her son from certain death. (Exodus 1:15-21) So, this mom did all she could do, and for three months she hid her baby!

Now, I don't know about your sons, but one of mine, in particular, had a very loud cry—a deep man-voice even as a baby. Hiding my infant son would have been very difficult.

I'm guessing it would not have been easy to keep Moses hidden and quiet either. But, she did hide him for as long as possible. And when she had done all she could do, **she placed him in the basket,** surrendering her precious son along with all of her own hopes and dreams for him.

Read the sequence of events that follow when she releases him. The King's daughter just happens to come to the river to bathe at that exact time. She just happens to see the basket. Her heart just happens to have compassion on that crying Hebrew baby. She just happens to ask his own sister to be his maid and has his own mother nurse him as she takes an illegal to be her own son. His life was spared!

These "happenings" are no mere coincidence. They are from the heart of a loving Father who stands by when we release our problems, fears, and concerns into His hands—the basket. He is always working on our behalf for our good, using all things. He is asking us to give our children, our husbands, our fears and concerns **to Him**—for our good and His glory.

What is your fear? Your heavy circumstance? Your focus? Can you release it?

Put it in the basket! Stand back and watch what happens when you trust God with all your concerns.

Oh, Father, fears are overtaking me. I'm trying to figure out how to discipline my kids, pay the next bill, love my husband, deal with my mom, siblings, neighbor and all the other issues in life that overwhelm me. Give me courage today to release these things to You. I make a conscious choice to give them into Your loving hands—the basket. Give me the patience to sit back with my hands off, and eyes to see Your mighty power at work. I trust You.

Scripture readings:

- Exodus 2:1-10
- Exodus 14:13
- Psalms 20
- Psalms 25
- Romans 8:28

Currently, what is your greatest fear or distraction that needs to be placed in the "basket"?

Are you willing to lay it down, or do you believe you can handle it better by yourself? Be honest

Do you believe God will take care of your concerns in His way and in His time, and His way will work for good in your life and the lives of those you love?

Is there evidence in your life that you are not trusting Him with your fears? Explain.

8

OVERWHELMED

Overwhelmed. This is a mom on any given day. And guess what? We are in great company!

Look at Mark 6:31-34:
Then Jesus said, "Let's go off by ourselves to a quiet place and rest awhile." He said this because **there were so many people coming and going that Jesus and his apostles didn't even have time to eat.**

Jesus went through it too. He understands.

So they left by boat for a quiet place, where they could be alone. **But many people** *recognized them and saw them leaving, and people from many towns ran ahead along the shore and* **got there ahead of them.**

Sound familiar? Like your life on any given day? Jesus was overwhelmed too.

He was human.

And He was God.

Jesus saw the huge crowd as he stepped from the boat, and he had compassion on them because they were like sheep without a shepherd. So he began teaching them many things.

Even Jesus knew the need to get away. And we need that time away too. Coffee with a friend once a week for an hour will refresh you. A regular date time with your husband can change your outlook.

But, the reality is that the crowd will be there when you get back. I think Jesus knew that and accepted it. How else would compassion rise in His heart?

Oh, Father. I know You were human, like me, and You were able to overcome the stress and press of people through compassion. I pray that You will grow compassion in my heart, even right at this moment for my own "crowd." The days are long, and people tell me the years are short, though today it seems like I will be at this forever! May my strength come from the joy of living for You, even when all seems like a mess around me. May Your compassion and example be mine, as I teach my children of Your unfailing love.

Scripture readings:

- Psalms 28:6-9
- Psalms 62
- Colossians 3:12
- Isaiah 54:10

Are you trying to do this mom thing in your own strength? What evidence do you have?

Are you strong or weak in compassion?

What would you say is the opposite of compassion?

Are you often looking for an escape? Can you identify ones you reach for? Are your escapes healthy for you and your family? List them and explain.

What things can you put in place to assure you can keep a healthy mind and heart? Is there someone who you might ask to hold you accountable?

God said this once and for all;
how many times have I heard it repeated?
"Strength comes straight from God."

Psalms 62:11 MSG

9

CHOOSE YOUR THOUGHTS

"I think I'm losing it!"

Come on, you know you've said it, or at least thought it more than once since you took on the title of Mom. I know I did. I still do, on any given day.

The mind of a wife and mother has about a million things tumbling around all at the same time. *Get your shoes on, we need to leave in ten minutes. What do you mean you can't find your shoes? (Why can't I find a system to teach my kids to put everything in place?) Where did I put my phone? Wait. Do I have all I need on my grocery list? What time was that appointment? Why is there no gas in my car?* I could go on all day.

Our minds are very complex, and let's admit it, we are pretty good at multitasking and getting a lot accomplished just through our thinking.

But, our minds are also the place we get tripped up.

I'm not enough. I'm too much. I'm a failure. I'm ugly and fat.

We have a very real enemy out to destroy us and our influence. When we have so many jumbled thoughts, we start hearing the lies more than believing the truth of who we are and Who He is.

The Bible is very clear on this: **If we belong to Christ, we have His mind!** (1 Corinthians 2:16) Not human wisdom, but the power of God.

That thought blows my mind. We have been given the mind of the Almighty? The Creator of heaven and earth? Let that sink in.

We **can** choose our thoughts! We **can** reject the lies of the enemy and agree with the Truth of our loving Father. We **can** set our mind on things above--where Christ is.

Jesus, I pray that my mind will be set on You, not on my human understanding. From here, things seem a little bleak and overwhelming. Will You help me set my mind on the things above and not on what I see and feel?

Scripture readings:

- 1 Corinthians 2
- 2 Corinthians 4:17-18
- 2 Corinthians 10:4-5
- Colossians 3:1-2
- Philippians 4:8
- Romans 12:2
- 1 Peter 1:13

Have you ever considered that you can change your thoughts?

What are three lies the enemy wants you to believe about yourself? List them in your journal.

What do you need to do to counter those lies? Spend some time thinking about this question.

How can you set your mind on things above rather than on your circumstances?

May all my thoughts be pleasing to him;
For I rejoice in the Lord.

Psalms 104:34

10

EMOTIONS

Is it that time of the month? Are your emotions getting the best of you today and causing your family to receive the worst?

Emotions. All the feels. Ugh. Some days it's really hard being a woman.

Yet, these very emotions were given us by God. It's part of His Divine nature imparted to us when He formed us in His likeness. For most of us women, nurturing, comforting, and tenderness are just a part of who we are. But those wonderful, deep-felt emotions can quickly turn into controlling, nagging, and freaking out.

Last time I checked, freaking out did not make the list as a fruit of God's Spirit.

Our emotions are not something to shy away from but are qualities to be developed by the guidance and leading of the Holy Spirit. Too many times we let our strong emotions take the lead and the winner is satan. The fall-out from these emotions leaves devastation and destruction for our family and in our own hearts.

In these moments, the strength and power of God are available for our asking. He is more than enough to help us overcome our weaknesses, and His grace is enough to cover the darkness of our hearts.

When you know your emotions are heightened, humble yourself before your family by telling them you realize you may not be in the best frame of mind. Ask for their forgiveness before you lose the battle. Armed with their understanding, and your own, you can face the hardest of days knowing He is in control, even of your feelings.

Father, sometimes it's really hard being a woman. Sometimes I don't even know if You really understand since You came as a man. But, since You are God and I'm not, I choose to trust You even with that. I admit my emotions tend to lead me some days, and the path is littered with hurt feelings and wounded hearts—even my own. I now place my emotions at Your feet. I know I'll need to do it again tomorrow and the day after, but I want to give You that control. Please keep me alert to the times when my emotions are teetering toward my human nature rather than Your Spirit. I choose YOU and your ways.

Scripture readings:

- Galatians 5:22-25
- Proverbs 15:13
- Proverbs 25:28
- Proverbs 29:11
- Ephesians 6:13
- Isaiah 30:15
- 2 Timothy 1:7

How often do you allow your feelings to take the lead? Never? Occasionally? Daily? Be honest.

What is the effect on your family when you allow your negative emotions to lead you? Explain

What is the effect on you? Write it out.

Do you believe your feelings can be led by His Spirit? Why or why not? Explain in your journal.

How easy is it to apologize to your family when you've allowed your emotions to take control? If this is difficult, what hinders you from honestly apologizing?

What actions can you put into place that might allow God to lead you rather than letting your feelings take control?

Please, God, rescue me!
Come quickly, Lord, and help me.

Psalms 70:1

11

DREAD

So, it's Monday. Or an upcoming holiday, or even just another hard day at work or with raising your crew. You are already dreading it. I've been there plenty of times. Being a mom is hard.

It may be when your husband is away from home, or even home, sick. Or, when you have to see your own mother. Or, you have to go back to work. Or, maybe it's when your kids wake up, your teen's pushback has you on edge and your hard day begins all over again.

Guess who is standing near at those times? Yep, your enemy. He knows your buttons, your vulnerable places. He loves dread. He is waiting and watching nearby to make sure you are disappointed, disillusioned, and discouraged. See the *dis-es*? He wants to remove you from your position.

Your position and place were given to you by your Creator. He knew just the right location on Earth and the perfect time in eternity to place you so you could bring Him the most glory. Guess what? It's right now, where you are! It's the very thing you are doing. It's being a mom, a wife, a daughter, a friend.

If your enemy removes you from that place and brings dread to that position, he has won. He has displaced and dis-appointed you from the very spot God has planted you for His glory!

Is it possible the fearful anticipation of what is ahead could be holding back the power of God from your pressing situations? Could you replace that dread with joyful expectation, believing that He is all you need and His power is shown even in your weaknesses?

Could His power within you do abundantly more than you could ever think or imagine if you stopped dreading what might happen and began expecting Him to work and show Himself mighty?

It could be a great paradigm shift.

Oh, Father. The dread of what is upcoming is overwhelming my thoughts and spilling over into my attitudes. My fears are holding back Your power in my own heart! I want to move out of Your way, to allow You to go before me. I want to replace the dread with expectation of all I know You can do in this place and time. Help me watch for You, to hope for You, to know You are at work even if I don't see it. I place my hand in Yours, knowing that resisting You is exactly what my enemy desires. Help me stand firm against him by choosing You. I'm expectant and excited to see what happens!

Consider reading the following scriptures from The Passion Translation (TPT). Find it on bible.com

- Luke 21:19
- John 16.33
- Acts 17:26
- 1 Corinthians 15:58
- 2 Corinthians 12: 8-10
- Ephesians 3:20
- Ephesians 6:10-13

In general, what do you most dread?

What emotions and attitudes are displayed in you when you are feeling that anticipation and fear?

Do you believe His presence, peace, and power are enough to overcome your feelings?

What can you do to watch expectantly for Him?

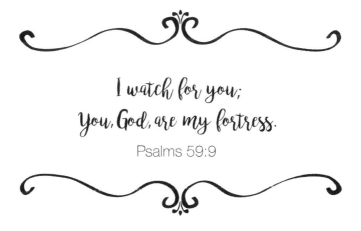

I watch for you;
You, God, are my fortress.

Psalms 59:9

12

MIRRORS OR LIGHTS?

When you have several children you have the opportunity for do-overs in parenting, thank God. Our poor oldest kids had a mom who focused on behavior modification. I naively believed if I taught them all the things *not* to do, and said it often enough, they would never choose to do wrong things. Crazy, I know now.

I was raising my kids to my standards—mirrors, reflecting what I thought was right or wrong. It didn't go well, as they pushed back against the rules and restrictions I tried to put in place for "right" living. The worst thing was, my heart was full of pride. I thought I knew all the right things to do and say if only they'd just listen to me.

God used my children to do a work in my heart. Through the conflicts, I began to see that a life of freedom isn't found in what we don't do. That is a spirit of religion. A life of freedom is about who He is in us and who we are becoming through Him—a living relationship.

As my relationship with Christ became more and more about Who He is and who I am in Him, my approach in training my children changed, too.

From this heart-change, I learned to not focus on all the frightening sins they might fall prey to: pornography, drugs, alcohol, swearing, deceit, sexual promiscuity, etc. Rather, we talked about the consequences of living in deliberate independence from God, sin that would harm our connection to Him, and the joy and freedom that come from a loving relationship with a living God.

Changing perspective also brought me relief and freedom in my parenting. I realized I didn't have the impossible responsibility of raising shiny, well-behaved, mirror-children. Instead, my calling was to direct them toward a personal relationship with the giver of Life. Following Jesus was *their* choice, not something I could control, no matter how much I tried. It was risky. It was living with faith in God, and not faith in myself.

As I released my children to Him, there were many bumps in the road as they worked out their own faith. But I have good news for you: each one of my kids has chosen to be a light for Jesus, not a mirror of their mom.

If you recognize yourself in these words, I encourage you to show your children the love and freedom that comes from intimately knowing Jesus, and the best way is to live it out in your own life. Your children will eventually want that relationship for themselves.

If you didn't have the chance to change your parenting along the way, it's never too late to apologize to your grown children for what you didn't know. Your humility and vulnerability just might open the door to some healing conversations.

Father, I admit this is a tough thing for me to consider. I don't want my children to go through hard things, especially some of the things I chose when I was younger. I pray that You give me wisdom to know what boundaries to put in place, but mostly for the wisdom to demonstrate your love and life to my children. I pray that they choose You and I pray that my example to them will be one that reflects your glory. May I raise Light-bearers and not mirrors of myself.

Scripture readings:

- Genesis 1:27
- Proverbs 22:6
- Romans 5:1-2
- Romans 6:11-18
- Romans 8:6-8
- 2 Corinthians 3:17-18
- Galatians 5:16-25

Is your parenting more focused on pointing your kids to Jesus or making them follow your rules? Think through recent encounters with your children.

What troubles in your children's lives are you trying to avoid? List them.

Do you believe strict rules will keep your children safe and under control? Based on your past experiences, how effective were rules in keeping you from making poor choices? Explain in your journal.

What is your motive in training your children? Fear of wrong choices? Appearances? Good grades? Behavior modification? Or are you focused on directing them to your loving Father?

Do you need to make adjustments? If so, what adjustments will you make?

In the image of God he created them
Genesis 1:27

13

JUST SMILE

Strength and dignity are her clothing,
And she smiles at the future. Proverbs 31:25

Smiling at the future. How does this Proverbs 31 woman possibly smile at what is to come? How does she have peace, even with the future?

Really think about it. None of us even know what tomorrow will bring. Some of us are planners—we like to know what's ahead so we can be prepared and ready for whatever may come. And when we don't know, fears can quickly surface.

Some of the fears I deal with and have dealt with in the past are for my kids' lives or my husband's life. In the days before cell phones, I had my husband's funeral planned out before he arrived home late from work! Fear is a very common thing with women.

I still have to fight the fear that something might happen to my family. That my health will deteriorate. Then where would I be? How would I make it? How could I survive?

So, what is this Proverbs 31 woman's secret? How can

she possibly smile at the unknown?

I believe she has complete trust in God's faithfulness and sovereignty. She trusts that He is in control no matter what comes, which brings her true peace.

She knows the source of those fears, and it isn't God. So, she smiles. She smiles at the future, knowing it's in His capable hands and that He is trustworthy. Her security is in Him.

I still want to get there—to that peaceful place where I can rest and trust and just smile. And most days, it is becoming easier. Some days, I still have to force that smile by believing the Truth of God's Word. My mind just has a hard time wrapping my heart completely around it.

One of my favorite authors, Corrie ten Boom, who lived through the horrible atrocities of the Holocaust, said, *"Never be afraid to trust an unknown future to a known God."* And, *"Worry does not empty tomorrow of its sorrow, it empties today of its strength."* She should know.

How about you? What fears are draining your strength and keeping you from smiling at the future? Confess those now. He has you, and your children.

Believe it.

Oh, Father. I want to know You, to trust You, to surrender even tomorrow into Your loving, sovereign hands, but I know my fears keep me bound and prevent me from trusting You fully. I ask for courage to make the constant choice to be wholly Yours, knowing You have my future, and my family's, in Your wise hands. May joy for who You are rise in my spirit right now, putting a smile on my face. Thank you for loving me, especially when I am fearful.

For a fresh perspective, consider reading these scriptures from The Passion Translation (TPT):

- Proverbs 31:25
- Psalms 28:7
- Psalms 32:8
- Psalms 91
- James 4:7

How secure are you about the future for yourself?
How secure are you about the future for your children. Explain or journal your answers.

How well do you know the attributes of God? Name as many as you can and keep a running list.

Could a better understanding of Who God is enable you to trust Him with the future? If so, what actions will you take to learn Who He is?

Who is God to you? Write it out.

14

WORDS ARE ETERNAL

"Sticks and stones may break my bones, but words will never hurt me!" Whatever. Our childish retort was a lie and we knew it. Words can hurt.

Words matter.

Words are powerful. God created the heavens and the earth by His Words. He *is* the Word! Words are important because they are the way we communicate with each other. We should know since the average woman is said to speak about 13,000 more words a day than a man! Words, whether spoken or silent, are also the way we communicate with God.

Words reveal our motives and intentions: whether spoken tenderly to comfort, bless, and encourage or in an explosion of anger to blame, defend, and convince. All of these words come from the same mouth, sometimes on the same day, often within a matter of moments. All words originate in our heart, and either build up or tear down. We can drown people, especially our families, with too many words or starve them by shutting down or withholding our uplifting words.

Words are eternal. We can never take back something we said, even if we say it in jest. There is always an element of truth in sarcasm, and sarcasm is a poor way to communicate with those we love, though our kids seem to draw that from us with their attitudes.

Even after the most heartfelt apology for our heated, hateful, or careless words, the destruction will always remain. It takes a mighty working of the Holy Spirit to heal wounds that are left from those words. You know. You've been on the receiving end. And often, you are the one on the giving end.

The Word of God teaches us that words originate in our hearts, reveal its condition, and have the power of life or death. Wow! That's a lot to consider. What are we leaving behind with our words? They are eternal.

May we speak fewer words to others, and more words to God.

Father, I confess that currently, my heart may not be in the best condition, considering my words. I repent of the harshness of my tone, the sharpness of my commands, and words that bring death and destruction rather than life and encouragement. I ask You to be the dwelling Presence of my heart today and always, being quick to remind me when I've displaced You with my own agenda and selfishness. May my words be a blessing to my family and others today, but especially to You. Thank You for loving me, even in my weaknesses.

Consider reading these scriptures from The Passion Translation (TPT):

- Matthew 12:33-37
- Matthew 15:8-10
- Matthew 15:17-20
- James 3:2-12
- Proverbs 18:21
- Proverbs 26:17-28
- Ephesians 4:29
- Psalms 141:3

"Words are eternal." Write in your journal the implications this statement has for you.

Based on what comes out of your mouth, what do your words reveal about the conditions of your heart?

Do you recall a time or specific words you used that were harsh, critical, hurtful or unnecessary? Prayerfully consider apologizing to those recipients and asking their forgiveness.

Are you speaking words of life? Explain.

Do you need to speak less often? More quietly? What about your tone of voice? Do you need to listen more than you speak? How might your family or friends answer this question about you? Write in your journal.

Write your own prayer asking God to help you be more self-aware and God-aware about what comes from my mouth.

15

THERMOSTAT

Getting up on cold mornings is really hard when we'd rather stay in our warm beds under the toastiness of our blankets. I remember winters when I'd race down the hall to turn the thermostat to a higher number.

As moms, our days often begin like this. Our kids have already set the "thermostat" for our morning, sometimes before we get out of bed. "Mom! I'm in a hurry to leave!" "Mom! He hit me!" "Mom! Tell her to stop!" We are left with the cold starkness of an overwhelming day, and it's only just begun.

Our inner thermostat begins to rise—not to a comfortable temperature, but to one that exceeds our own comfort. If we aren't careful, the steam we are holding in may explode over the entire household.

Guess what, mama? You are the one in control of the thermostat of your home. I know…there are too many things thrown at you, coming against you and your peace. But, I have learned that we moms have the power to set the tone for our household.

What is your response when those "mommmms" start coming your way? What is your reaction when your teen's attitude is less than stellar? Do you stoop to his or her level, reacting with anger and heightened emotions? Or do you rise above, responding with quietness, firmness, and calmness? It seems like a really tall order, but scripture tells us we have the fruit of God's Spirit living in us. Love, peace, kindness…

Why do we so quickly forget? Why do we let our kids set the tone? Why do we allow the enemy to win, day in and day out?

Jesus called us to be peace*makers*, choosing to set the tone for our day; not peace*keepers* who sweep our attitudes under the rug along with the breakfast crumbs. Peacemakers take the needed time to make hard, right choices, instead of defaulting to their natural inclinations and ease. Peacekeepers shut up and shut down, hoping everything will eventually blow over on its own yet become disappointed when it doesn't happen.

Mamas, we have His Spirit within us enabling us to establish the mood of our homes with our attitudes and words. Knowing our attitudes speak louder than our words, we will let our kids know that we choose to have a good day, no matter what comes. We will not allow the enemy to overtake and consume us. We will choose love, patience, and self-control. We will choose Him!

Oh Father, give me the ability to see past the chaos of our mornings, our days. Help me set my mind on You, and to draw on Your peace and presence to be the best example of You to my children today. Help me set the tone for the day, the entire day, remembering that You have gone before me and have prepared a way for every circumstance that arises, even those that threaten to take me down. Thank You for your Spirit who never leaves me. I choose You right now. Your presence makes me smile, no matter what is ahead.

Scripture readings:

- Galatians 5:22-25
- Matthew 5:9
- Deuteronomy 31:8
- Isaiah 30:15
- Isaiah 45:2
- Psalms 77:19

How well do you set a positive tone in your home? What is the evidence? Write it out.

Peacemaking is much harder than peacekeeping. What hurdles prevent you from being a peacemaker?

What specific triggers tempt you to lose your patience? List them.

What are some things that can be adjusted to enable you to set a better emotional tone in your home? (Eliminating children or husbands is not allowed on this list!)

16

OPPORTUNITIES?

"You guys are making me crazy!" I know you've said it in elevated decibels to your children at least once. Probably several times. I know, because I yelled it many times to my own kids. The bickering, tattling, sassy and disrespectful attitudes, and constant needs agitate us to the point of pulling out our hair—or screaming at everyone. When the dust settles, we don't feel any better. Sure, there's a moment of quietness, until this scenario repeats itself.

What might happen next time if you are ready with a different perspective? What if you began to see that frustrating situations are actually the hand of God in your life, and in the lives of your children?

He is giving you opportunities to make hard, right choices of love, patience, and self-control; to choose Him. He is presenting you with teachable moments for your children, and for your own heart. He is giving you occasions to become more like Him.

He is giving special moments to teach your children that anxiety can be controlled by the power of the Holy Spirit living in you—and it begins with controlling yourself. Sure, you'll forget. Often your frustrations will win. When that happens, stop, pray, invite Christ into the situation, and try again.

As you practice seeing an "opportunity" rather than just another frustrating time of disappointment and discouragement, you will begin to see growth and change in your heart that will spill over onto your children. Try it! Press through and don't give up.

Father, I confess that I lose it all too often with my kids. The explosion of words and commands I yell don't make any of us feel peaceful or good. I pray that You will help me remember to recognize these times as opportunities to show You honor by choosing the fruit of Your Presence rather than an explosion of hurtful words. I invite You, right now, into the very first situation that presents itself, knowing that Your strength and power lives in me and that You will give me the right words of love, patience, and self-control needed for the moment. Thank You for Your patience with me.

Scripture readings:

- Exodus 4:12
- Psalms 28:6-7
- Matthew 7:12
- 1 Corinthians 13:4
- Galatians 5:22-23
- Philippians 4:6-7
- James 1:2-3
- 1 Peter 1:6-7

Is it possible for you to see conflicts as opportunities to show the attributes of God to your family?

Journal what you believe your loving Father is saying to you in these situations.

Does He see you? Does He understand? Is He with you?

Journal what you will do differently the next time you are overwhelmed in a situation and want to scream at your children. Picture it in your mind. How will you choose to respond?

See what great love the Father has lavished on us, that we should be called children of God! And that is what we are!

1 John 3:1

17

YOU AREN'T ENOUGH

How will I ever be able to teach my kids all they need to know? What if I have them in the wrong school, or missed a sport they might have excelled in? What if they were supposed to be a musician and we didn't have the means for them to take lessons? What if I'm not enough for them? What if I ruin them?

You are the mom. You are supposed to be there for them and make sure they go in the right direction and don't fail. Right?

Our unending fear and anxiety over being "just the right mom," covering all the bases, and providing the right opportunities is exhausting. We find ourselves hoping they won't have to spend their adult years on a therapist's sofa because of us. It's all overwhelming and leaves us questioning the future.

Somehow, we've been conditioned to believe a mom is *everything* and we should be perfect—Pinterest perfect. We know our own moms couldn't meet that expectation, yet we have the idea that *we* will be different. Better.

Hold on, I have news for you: **you aren't enough.**

Did the air just leave your lungs? Take a deep breath and say it with me, "I am not enough for my kids."

And that's okay. It's more than okay, and this is why: if we were enough for our kids, they would have no need for Jesus! We were given our children for a short time to demonstrate his love to them, to teach them his ways, and to raise them in the way they should go —toward him! It's a high calling, greater than most any other.

The best news for us is that He loves our children even more than we do, which seems impossible. He will be the One who makes sure they will learn all they need, have all they need and be all they need. Because **He is enough!**

Now, hopefully, this realization and declaration offers you some newfound freedom! Post it on a note to view often: **I am not enough, but He is!** May you stop beating yourself up and carrying your guilt, and instead, begin walking in freedom today.

Father, thank You for being enough. Help me rest in that truth, believing that You have gone before me and are making a way for my children, even now. Help me live in the freedom that ***I am not enough, but that You are more than enough!*** *May Your peace and presence flood my heart as I rest in You, trusting You with the future of my children.*

Scripture readings:

- Deuteronomy 31:8
- Isaiah 46:3-4
- Psalms 68:19
- Proverbs 22:6
- Ephesians 3:20-21
- Philippians 4:19
- 2 Peter 1:3

How hard do you push yourself in trying to be "super mom"? Explain in your journal

Does the thought of not being enough for your children bring you freedom? Explain why or why not.

Do you truly believe God can give your children all all they need? Why or why not? Journal your thoughts.

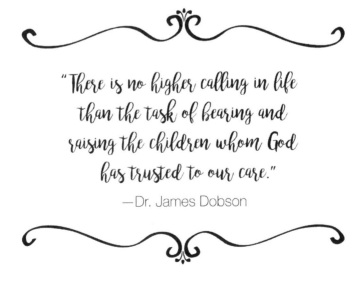

"There is no higher calling in life than the task of bearing and raising the children whom God has trusted to our care."

—Dr. James Dobson

18

PRESSURE

A while back I took my four youngest grandsons, ages ranging 5-10, to a local drive-in restaurant. It was a date with Mimi! On this sunshiny day, we sat outside while they enjoyed their slushes. The bantering and chatter quickly turned to fart jokes, because…boys.

To work off some of their sugary energy, we found a long curb and used it to invent games, which naturally became competitions. The area was a little trashy, and one of my grands stomped on a discarded juice box. Simultaneously, another grand ran by at just the right moment to have old juice sprayed all over his foot. Riotous laughter ensued.

Pressure always squeezes out what is inside.

For us, the pressure may be from overcommitments. Sometimes, it's just the regular, overwhelming daily tasks and family relationships that seem to be more than we can bear. The pressure is on to get it all done. To get to work on time with a good attitude. To serve a meal three times a day! The constancy of keeping clothes and floors and bathrooms clean. Dealing with toddler tantrums or teen attitudes. Digging deep to be receptive to intimacy with our husband.

When pressures come, whatever is inside gets squeezed out, contaminating everyone near us. The contents of our hearts is exposed, and it isn't lovely.

Now, rather than having a guilt trip here, let's talk about that junk. It's out for all to see, so what will you do about it now? Stuff it back in and wait for the next high-pressure time to expose you all over again? Or will you recognize the sin, naming it for what it really is: pride, fear, or control? Will you allow the light of His presence to shine in your dark heart?

This is an opportunity. Will you waste it? Confess the sin that explodes from you and move forward. The next time pressure comes you will be on guard. No smelly, old juice will rule your heart!

Father, my life is full of pressure. Sometimes, one more thing added to my already-too-full day sends me into a full-on explosion and the result is not pretty. I confess this sin in my heart and ask You to give me the courage and boldness to allow You to lead my heart with Your love. I know some of my pressure is self-inflicted so I ask You to reveal to me the areas I can trim away to lighten my load. Give me courage to choose the significant over the urgent, the eternal over the fleeting. Help me to breathe You in, recognizing that this is just one more opportunity to choose You.

Consider reading these scriptures from The Message:

- Proverbs 24:10
- Matthew 11:28-30
- Ephesians 4:22-24
- James 1:2-6
- James 1:12-25
- John 8.34-36

Sometimes, even good things in our lives need to be dropped so we can live with the best. What are things in your life that you and **only** you can do as mom and wife? Make a list in your journal.

Is it difficult for you to say "no" to activities that maybe aren't the best idea for this season in your life?

Do the things that take up your time have eternal value? Put a star next to those that do.

In reviewing your schedule and retaining the activities that are truly significant to your family, are there things that could be eliminated or delegated to relieve some of the pressure in this season? Pray over your list, asking God to reveal His activities for you.

Are you teaching your children to do age-appropriate household chores, or are you trying to do everything by yourself? Explain your thoughts.

Will you show this list to your husband for further insight? If not, take some time to consider why.

19

PRESSED

I came across a poem by Annie Johnson Flint many years ago when my kids were young. Her words spoke truth to my overwhelming life. So I could remember them, I made a copy and had it taped to my closet mirror for years as a reminder that pressures *will* come over and over again. This woman learned how to handle the pressures, and her words were a great example to me.

Annie's life was full of difficulties. Her mother died after her younger sister was born. With no mother to raise them, her father gave the sisters to another family, the Flints, who both died when Annie and her sister were in their teens. Right out of high school, Annie wanted to teach, but arthritis crippled her. As a young woman in her twenties, now in a wheelchair, she was living her life dependent on others. Annie never married, nor was she a mother, but her life was full of more disappointments and discouragement than most of us will endure. Her life was very difficult. She was pressed. The question remains: what will we choose to do when that pressure or discouragement comes?

Pressures have a purpose.

Pressed so intensely it seems beyond strength;
Pressed in the body and pressed in the soul,
Pressed in the mind till the dark surges roll;
Pressed by foes, and pressured by friends;
Pressure on pressure, till life nearly ends;
Pressed into loving the staff and the rod,
Pressed into knowing no helper but God;
Pressed into liberty where nothing clings,
Pressed into faith for impossible things;
Pressed into living a life for the Lord,
Pressed into living a Christ-life outpoured.
~Annie Johnson Flint 1866-1932

Father, I long for the eternal, faith-filled outlook of Annie Flint. Give me eyes to see the pressures of life as real opportunities to exchange my disappointments for Your joy, and my discouragement as an occasion to bring You glory. May these words of hers be truth to my heart and a reminder that only through You will I find strength, freedom, and a life of purpose. Remind me today as the pressures come, that You fill all my needs.

Consider reading these scriptures from The Message:

- 1 Peter 1:6-7
- 2 Corinthians 4:5-18
- 2 Corinthians 12:7-10
- Psalms 16:5-11

Have you considered that pushing through the pressures in your life with the grace of God brings Him glory? Explain in your journal.

How will you choose to respond when the pressures come? Write it out.

Who do you know that handles the pressures of life well? Why do you think they handle pressures well?

Write them a note of encouragement today, telling them how they inspire you.

As pressure and stress bear down on me,
I find joy in your commands.
Psalms 119:143

20

MODEL IT

Kids are great at adding pressure to our day. All the questions, all the needs, all the conflicts. Life sure was easier before God added these blessings to our lives.

When siblings conflict, our mama antennas quickly rise like a red flag. We want it to stop! Now. Especially before it becomes physical, which it can, even when our children are young. The world calls this "sibling rivalry," but I like to think of it more as normal human interaction—human relationships.

Every relationship has conflict. Relationships would be easy if it weren't for the people! We chuckle at that statement, but we know it's true.

As moms, we find ourselves repeating our words over and over again: "Get along!" "Stop hitting your brother!" "What am I going to do with you two?" "Will it ever stop?" "Go to your room!" We ask the same unanswered questions and fire repeated commands, and it seems nothing changes.

We are faced with the very same issues today that we dealt with yesterday. We are weary from repeating the same words to deaf ears that just don't get it. We feel like broken records.

During Jesus' years of ministry, He repeated himself over and over, but never with one-sentence commands flung in desperation. He took time. He sat with people and had a chat with them. His stories were repetitious—about the same issues: loving God and loving others. He repeated himself to people who just didn't get it, but he didn't quit saying it. He just took a different tack, tried a different way.

He set a good example for us, saying what needed to be said in quiet, calm, creative repetition with love—not in screams and orders. He taught by example.

Here's the thing: only God can change a heart. If words changed a person's heart, all my kids would have been perfect!

Mamas, keep correcting in love, but more often than you speak, model a calm and quiet spirit. Take a moment to compose yourself and settle your nerves. Demonstrate an apology by asking their forgiveness when you lose your calm, and take the time to teach your kids to apologize to one another. Role-play a repeat of the heated scenario, asking for calmer attitudes and voices. Just don't fall apart and give up! Keep repeating and practicing. After all, how many times does the Bible tell us "do not fear"? And yet…

Today, begin taking the time to sit your kids down, not for a lecture, but a sharing of life and love and relationship. Pray with them and over them, pouring out your heart to God right in front of them. It won't be wasted time.

Don't just say it; model it. Don't just say it; pray it.

Father, I admit I lose it way too often when my kids conflict. Please help me make margin in my day to spend the time necessary to train them, teaching them Your love and Your ways in creative non-lectures. Help me listen to my own words as they flow from my heart, checking for lack of patience and kindness, but most of all, help me to not be a hypocrite of my own words. I pray for a glimmer of Your presence in my kids' hearts, showing me I am on the right path. Give me boldness to pray in front of them, making You the center of our day.

Consider reading these scriptures from The Message:

- Galatians 6:1-12
- Deuteronomy 6:4-9
- Matthew 5:1-10

How quick are you to apologize to your children when you lose your cool? Think about it.

Do you often feel like if you just said it enough, or the right way, then maybe your kids would understand and change their ways? Explain.

What prevents you from taking the time to work through a conflict? Journal your thoughts.

What is it that prevents you from stopping in the middle of a conflict and praying? Fear of what the children might think? Inability to pray "correctly"? Unbelief that anything will change? Write out those fears in your journal.

Spend some time searching for scriptural truth that counters those lies, copying them in your journal.

May the favor of the Lord our God rest on us; Establish the work of our hands for us—Yes, establish the work of our hands.

Psalms 90:17

21

DARK THOUGHTS

I've mentioned days of walking down our long drive to our rural mailbox with the thought of running away from the daily grind. I was longing for the sheer bliss of adult conversation, the thrill of leaving the bickering and conflicts behind, or the excitement of just going to the bathroom alone! You know, where little fingers don't appear under the door, or some kid isn't yelling at you to hurry up or come make a snack. Yes, you know what I'm talking about.

Occasionally, my thoughts of running away were not from my selfish desires and daydreams of a simpler life, but because I was convinced someone else would be more suitable to raise my family.

Losing my cool, raising my voice, not connecting well with my husband, all combined with hormonal days led me to be convinced that my family would certainly be better off without me. My family surely deserved someone other than me.

I never did leave, but I did entertain those thoughts long enough to head down a dark spiral of self-contempt and hatred, more than once.

Sleep deprivation, having more than we can do alone,

and the noise levels in our home can contribute to those dark thoughts. If we aren't careful, we will find ourselves in a bottomless pit of despair, wanting an "out" for our present life.

You understand. It's not uncommon among moms. How can we fight these despairing thoughts?

STOP them. Stay with me. First, simply stop. Period. Don't do anything. Don't take action. Don't call someone. Don't freak out. Stop!

TAKE all those dark, wandering thoughts captive. Immediately! Grab them before they run wild, making more out of what's going on than is really true. We are extremely proficient in allowing our thoughts to take us to the worst negative place possible. You have the power of God living in you, giving you the ability to stop those thoughts.

OBEY. Make your mind obedient to the Word of God. Apply His truth to your circumstances and thinking. Recall scriptures that counter your negative thoughts. Reach out and ask someone to help you with truths to counter the lies, or dig deep into God's word. Quickly recall your relationship with Jesus, remembering that as His daughter, you don't have to be ruled by negative patterns.

PLACE all your thoughts and circumstances at the feet of Jesus, waiting in expectation as you trust Him to work everything for your good and His glory, even when it doesn't seem possible.

S.T.O.P.! Stop, take, obey, place. Remember this acronym when you are headed down the dead-end road of negativity, bondage, and despair. You *can* overcome that spiral of defeat!

Father, I admit I have been on this road too many times. Sometimes, it seems as if life is too hard and I'm in the wrong place with the wrong people doing all the wrong things. Help me to STOP these negative thought patterns, knowing that You have placed me at this very time in history, with the very people who will shape me into who You desire me to be, even when I mess up. I want to choose perseverance and push through the tough times. I choose to STOP those thoughts, trusting all my circumstances and people to You. I wait expectantly to see You at work. Your patience with me is inconceivable. I praise You for Your love and grace—just for me!

Consider reading these scriptures from The Message:

- Matthew 10:29-30
- Psalms 30:8-12
- Psalms 143:7-10
- Psalms 34:17-20
- 2 Corinthians 1:8-9
- 2 Corinthians 10:3-6
- Romans 8:9-11

How often do you allow your mind to spiral down a negative or dark path? Is there anything that triggers your negative thinking? Spend some time thinking about this and journal your experiences.

Do you truly believe you are in control of your thoughts? Explain in your journal.

What will you do to help yourself remember to STOP before you allow your thoughts to spiral completely out of control? Write it out.

Do you believe He is working all things for your good? Explain why or why not.

O Lord, I cry out to you.
I will keep pleading day by day.

Psalms 88:13

22

ENCOURAGE YOURSELF

Did you wake up this morning feeling lonely despite your houseful of people? Are you feeling forgotten and unimportant, unappreciated and incompetent—like you can't do this anymore and no one even cares? Welcome to the mom club—the mom life. The Bible tells us children are a reward, and we so want to believe it, but motherhood rarely feels rewarding. Why is this calling one that leaves us feeling less-than and unfulfilled?

We are lacking, uninspired, and unmotivated. We need courage to face another day.

The Biblical character David was no mom, but he was a man that knew adversity. In 1 Samuel 30, we read that David, a mighty warrior, conquered some strong, powerful adversaries. What a great accomplishment! But, when he and his men came back to their city, they found it completely destroyed by fire and every family was taken captive. They were devastated. The men wept until there were no tears left.

After that, his own men turned on him and talked of stoning David. After all, he was the leader who made the decisions that led to this terrible outcome. In the moment we think David could have sunk into deep despair and resigned his leadership, the end of verse 6 says *"But, David found strength in the Lord his God."* King James Version says David encouraged himself. David added courage to himself!

Sometimes we may not have anyone around us to build us up—to add courage to our days. In fact, on many days we are ready to quit! But like David did, we can encourage ourselves. We can find strength in the Lord our God. He is there for the asking, giving us boldness and courage to face the next five minutes and the entire day.

Try it. Write yourself some encouraging notes and post them around the house, reminding you of the strength of your God. Draw strength from those truths today. Add courage to yourself!

Father, I am feeling less than, lonely, and unappreciated. I know my enemy waits right at those places and wants me to be defeated and discouraged. Please give me Your strength today and help me add courage to myself by choosing You and Your ways. Remind me today that You are there, You will never leave me, You are fighting my battles for me, and You love me more than I will ever realize this side of Paradise. May the joy of knowing You be my strength!

Scripture readings:

- Psalms 31:7-8
- Psalms 94:18-19
- Psalms 121
- Song of Solomon 7:10
- Romans 15:13
- Hebrews 4:15-16
- Hebrews 7:25

How often do you find yourself focusing on how unappreciated you are? Explain in your journal.

What happens when you allow that thought to travel?

What are three healthy things you can do when you're feeling lonely and unimportant? Write them down.

Which scriptures will you reach for when you need encouragement? List them.

Bend down, O Lord, and
hear my prayer; answer me,
for I need your help.

Psalms 86:1

23

ENCOURAGING WOMEN

What a wonderful thing it is to be a woman...unless you peek at social media. Then all hell breaks loose!

Immunizations or not? Natural childbirth or epidural? Home education or public school? Spanking or not? Breastfeeding or bottle? Baby-led weaning or spoon-fed? Speaking of food, we could list a page full of opinions and debates! Sugar-free, dairy-free, gluten-free, pesticide-free, nut-free, grass-fed, organic, low-fat, low-carb, GMO, BPA, MSG. Agh! It's too much.

We all have opinions, but often those opinions can alienate and separate friends. We are notorious for this. Our passions get the best of us, and soon we think others need to believe the way we do.

What if we allowed other women to be who they are? Rather than tearing down one another to make ourselves feel better, what might happen if we began to encourage and build up each other? What if we tried to understand another point of view? What if we quit sharing our self-righteous opinions with other women, and simply kept our thoughts to ourselves?

We want to be included in the conversation. We want

to be heard. But is it really worth it? We need to encourage one another in this gig called motherhood. We need each other to survive!

Today, I challenge you to call a girlfriend to offer uplifting words. The fastest way to encourage yourself is to encourage another.

Mail an actual handwritten note instead of sending an email or quick text. Take her a favorite drink or latte and drop by for a quick hug, telling what a great mom she is. Make her a pot of soup or a casserole for her freezer. Offer to keep her kids for a date night with her husband.

Get creative and look for ways to add value to other women, other moms. Your uplifting words matter and the women in your life need to hear them. You will be amazed at the courage it will add to your own day.

Father, I know I've been caught up in conversations I should not have been, using my time for things of insignificance. I know my strong opinions may have been hurtful to others. May I never again tear down another to build myself up. I pray that my heart will be enlarged to know that words of encouragement have far greater worth than my opinion on any matter. Show me the right person to encourage today and prepare my heart to know just the right thing to do and say for her. I'm excited for the possibilities!

Consider reading these scriptures from The Passion Translation (TPT):

- Proverbs 11:25
- Proverbs 26:17
- Proverbs 26:20-23
- Proverbs 31:26

- 2 Corinthians 1:3-5
- Ephesians 4:29
- 1 Timothy 3:11

Why do you think most women have a difficult time encouraging one another? Explain in your journal.

How prone are you to gossip? When or where does it seem to happen? Journal about this.

How often do you share your opinions with others without first being asked? Is this beneficial or detrimental to yourself and others? Explain in your journal.

Who is on your heart to encourage today? Write them a note right now.

Are there people in your circle of influence who could benefit from your regular encouragement? Name them.

How would it benefit you to make a practice of encouraging other women? Explain.

Kind words are like honey—
sweet to the soul and healthy to the body.

Proverbs 16:24

OVERWHELMED BY MY BLESSINGS

24

ENCOURAGE YOUR CHILDREN

When is the last time you remember encouraging your child? Think about it.

I'll admit. This was not a strength of mine. Positivity and encouragement are things I had to work at.

I was great at telling my kids to clean their room, tie their shoes, get their feet off the sofa. I often said, "Lower your voice!" "Please do not sing that song one more time!" "Get your shoes on!" "Hurry, we are late!" "Stop arguing!" I was great at commands, demands, and reprimands. It took years of practice for me to learn to really encourage my children.

Does this sound familiar? How often do you really encourage—add courage—to your children?

Ask yourself, *what does my child need to hear from me?* What fears or lies is he believing, even at a young age? What obstacle is my teen facing? What words of courage and confidence can I speak that might help her face the trials of these tough years?

Have you become so accustomed to the daily grind of "mom-ing," you may have forgotten how to take the time to encourage your children? Remember: **the way you speak to your children will become the way they speak to themselves.** What a sobering thought.

So, let's make a plan. This idea is so foreign and forgotten for some that you may need to write a few statements down. Here are some examples to get you started:

"I am so proud of the way you handled that conflict with your sister."

"Wow! I love it when you mow the lawn with such care! You are so responsible."

"I noticed that you did your chores without having to be asked. You are really maturing!"

"Your strength of character shows when you deal with tough friendship issues. I sure am proud to be your mom."

"It was so sweet of you to share your candy with your brother. You have such a giving heart."

"Great attitude!"

"Thank you for your respect."

"Cool outfit!"

Praise your child's character development, not their perfection. Your words of encouragement will carry them farther than you realize, and you will begin to see new maturity. I promise!

Father, I admit that in the process of trying to train my children, my words have become more about what to do or not do rather than positive words of encouragement. I ask for new thoughts—new creative ideas to feed my children with life-giving words of affirmation. Remind me when I slip back into old patterns of commands and instructions. I fight against the mommy-guilt that wants to consume me for recognizing this weakness in my heart, deciding instead to choose words that will build up and strengthen my children. I know You will provide those words to me as I listen to Your heart. Thank You for Your unfailing love.

Scripture readings:

- Psalms 127:3-5
- Proverbs 12:25
- Proverbs 18:21
- Colossians 2:2-3
- 1 Thessalonians 5:11
- Hebrews 10:24

Were you own parents encouraging to you as a child? Did your mom build you up or not?

What was the benefit of that encouragement from your parents? What detriments did the lack of encouragement have on your life? Write it out.

What creative ideas can you put into place to ensure that you will encourage your children? List the ways.

What things do each of your children need to hear from you? List their names and the qualities you can encourage in each of them.

she gives instructions with kindness

Proverbs 31:26

25

ENCOURAGING MEN

Encouraging the men who are in our lives can help them believe in themselves.

Maybe you've been at this marriage thing for a while. Like being a mom, it may not be going quite the way your fairytale dreams imagined. For others of you, it didn't go well at all. Marriage is tough and works best when both partners are 100% invested.

If you are married and struggle to be encouraging, don't despair. It will get easier as you *determine* to encourage your husband. For those who have no husband, especially if your husband left his children, learn to build up and empower your sons to become legacy changers. The devastation left in their father's wake is not something you want your grandchildren to endure.

Fill your husband's or son's love-tank with your loving and kind words, your respect. Build him up. Give him injections of hope and courage, filling his mind and heart with your belief in him.

Here are some suggestions to get you thinking:

"Thank you for working so hard for our family. It means more to me than I say sometimes, but I wanted you to know that I do notice."

"Your quiet and calm spirit is just what I need. God knew when he brought you to me."

"I sure am glad you are so strong! I could have never moved that sofa without you."

"When you open the door for me, it makes me feel so loved and cherished."

Okay—these may not be your statements. In fact, your husband or son may be failing in many of these areas mentioned, or even more, but he still needs encouragement. While we know that nothing we say can change a heart, our harsh words can often leave a man feeling deflated. Don't fall into this trap:

"No, that's not how I do it."

"For the thousandth time, please put the seat down on the toilet!"

"Why do you always _____?"

"I wish you would _____."

"You are too rough and harsh with the kids."

These uninvited, critical statements pour from our mouth offering only dejection, discouragement, and disappointment to our men. And we wonder why our husbands and sons are becoming distant and won't open up to us anymore!

If this hits a nerve in your heart, please ask for forgiveness from your husband, son, or any man in your life. Be vulnerable and ask him to let you know when your words or statements hurt him.

Begin to add words of encouragement to your conversation with him daily. Slip notes into his briefcase or lunchbox. Text him throughout the day with kind words and thoughts, not with what just broke and who needs discipline or what he forgot to do. Remember to tell him all that he means to you. And, anytime you think of something positive to say, say it, right then!

Your mommy days will eventually come to an end, but hopefully, your wife days will continue. Cherish your man now so those future years together will be exciting and full of love and joy!

You single moms will begin a new season of life. Continue building up and encouraging your sons for a lasting relationship!

Married moms: *Father, I know I'm not always good at encouraging my husband and sometimes it is truly hard to find positive things to praise. After taking care of the kids and the house, or being at work all day, I am often left with nothing for him and I catch myself demanding and commanding, rather than building him up. I confess this to You and pray for an open heart and mind, retraining myself to offer encouragement to him. Give me boldness and the humility to admit my failings to him and the courage to set things right. I know You will show me the way.*

Single moms: *Father, you and I both know encouragement wasn't easy for me, as it was sometimes difficult to find anything positive to say. I pray that the broken legacy of my past will not be carried along to my children. May my words for them be uplifting and encouraging, reminding them of who they are and Who You are for them. May You be their Father, and may You be my Husband. (Isaiah 54:5) Thank You for Your love that never fails.*

Scripture readings:

- Psalms 141:3
- Proverbs 14:1
- Proverbs 16:24
- Proverbs 19:13
- Proverbs 21:9
- Proverbs 31:10-12
- Ecclesiastes 4:9-12
- 1 Peter 3:1-2

How encouraging are you to the men in your life?

Write down at least three positive things you admire about your husband.

Write down three or more positive things about your son(s) next to their name.

Do you send more texts of love and encouragement to your husband, or more about what is wrong and the bad day you're having? Think carefully.

Send your husband or son a loving, encouraging text right now, and set a reminder on your phone to do this more often.

List out some respectful statements you will say to your husband. (You may need to dig deep for this).

Are you brave enough to ask the men in your life if they feel respected by you? If not, why?

The humble will see their God at work and be glad.
Let all who seek God's help be encouraged.

Psalms 69:32

26

INTERRUPTIONS

We'd be sitting at the table doing school, all my children together, fairly focused. That's a win! Then, a knock at the back door. Grr! It happened almost daily. My neighbor would be bringing me a plant from her yard, or fresh lettuce from her garden, or a trinket to share. I would quickly thank her, try to hurry the conversation along, all the while hoping my kids would still be at the table when I came back.

My scheduled day and routine had been interrupted, and this mama was **not** happy. I'm certain I brought my exasperation back to the table while rounding up my kiddos to teach them math and reading.

Looking back, I can see a missed opportunity. That knock at my door was an interruption to me, but I now realize from God's view, this was a planned visitation. This "interruption" was an appointment sent for me to learn patience, practice love, and teach my children by example.

He used this for good in my life because He wastes nothing. In that moment, I think I missed the real lesson and especially failed in sharing it with my children.

Interruptions are what we name the unexpected events in our personal routine and agenda. That time you had to stop what you were doing to run your husband's work key to his office. When your mom phoned at just the wrong time. When you woke up sick or even worse—when your husband comes home sick. When the car needs gas and you are late to work. The potty accidents, the temper tantrums, the spills.

What if we began asking God what He has for us in these interruptions? What if we began seeing the fracturing of our schedule as a gift sent to shape and grow us? What if we stopped in the moment and asked God to show us the lesson? What if we shared with our children what we are learning in that moment, rather than sharing our huffy exasperation?

Then, maybe God's agenda could become our new agenda. Perhaps the shift in plans is an opportunity to speak to our children about grace and kindness and a life lived for God rather than living for ourselves. This can become a time to adjust our timetable, rather than being irritated and hateful.

With a new mindset and perspective change, we can begin calling those troublesome interruptions "Divine Appointments" instead. Will we allow Him to be in charge of our day?

Father, You know I like my day to have order and purpose. I pray that my idea of order and my own purposes will never overrule Your plan for my day. When my schedule is altered, help me to be extremely alert and aware that You are very near and have a new plan that is far better than my own, even when it doesn't seem possible. Help me recognize my exasperation as a signal that I am straying from Your presence and peace. From now on I choose to call these interruptions "Divine Appointments"!

Scripture readings:

- Psalms 25:4-11
- Isaiah 55:8-13
- Isaiah 58:9-12
- 1 Corinthians 13:5
- Philippians 4:4-9
- James 1:2-4

Is sticking to a schedule important to you? Why or why not? Explain in your journal.

Does the term "Divine Appointments" change your perception of interruptions?

What might this new perspective change for you? Explain.

Writing it out is important so you can look back later and see how much you have grown.

27

VISION CORRECTION

Recently I got a new prescription for contacts. I could no longer read words on the TV or in movies, and I often missed recognizing someone at a distance. Having the correct lenses made everything better!

Most of us need *spiritual* vision correction.

Maybe our lens is criticism. We see the holes in the sofa rather than being grateful for a place to sit. We see how lazy our husband is at home rather than seeing how hard he really does work. We see our teen wasting his time and potential rather than seeing a growing, young heart. We focus on the messes more than making memories.

Maybe our lens is comparison. We see our friend has a nicer house or newer car than we do. We see someone with better behaved, smarter, or more athletic children than ours. We know a friend whose husband actually prays with her. She is in far better shape, her hair is prettier, her clothes are nicer.

Interestingly, when we see through the lenses of criticism and comparison, next comes complaining. We've lost our contentment, our joy, and our peace.

Complaining and discontentment come when we place our satisfaction in anything other than Jesus. He is the only thing that will never change. He is a solid place—the Rock—to stand on. When we fix our eyes on Him, suddenly we don't need vision correction! We have new eyes to see.

Our criticism, our comparison, and our complaining all fall away as we stand before a mighty God.

Here's the deal: we generally find what we are looking for. May our eyes be opened to see with new eyes, His eyes—goodness, provision, beauty, love!

Father, I confess I far too often see all the things that need to be changed rather than seeing all the great things and people You've placed in my life. I ask for forgiveness and repent before You. I pray that You will renew my mind and heart to begin to see things through Your eyes, recognizing all the good You have provided for me. May Your heart for others be the lens I look through rather than my criticism and comparison. I begin this day remembering to fix my eyes on You.

Scripture readings:

- Psalm 25:15
- Isaiah 35:3-6
- Matthew 13:13-17
- Matthew 6:22-23
- Acts 9:17-18
- 2 Corinthians 4:4
- Hebrews 12:1-3

Are you prone to criticism and fault-finding? What might be the reason(s)? What steps can you take to begin seeing more positively? Write it out.

Do you often compare yourself or your family to others? Why?

What insecurity do you need to identify and bring into the light? Write it down. Are there more?

Are you a complainer? What things or people are you expecting to bring you satisfaction? Name them.

Complaining can be silenced by gratitude. Write three things you're thankful for in your journal. Begin a list and add to it each day.

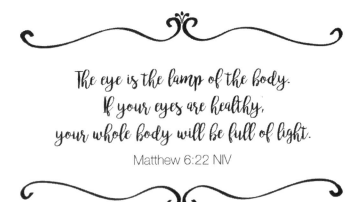

The eye is the lamp of the body.
If your eyes are healthy,
your whole body will be full of light.

Matthew 6:22 NIV

28

MOM GUILT

Mom guilt. It's a universal feeling. It washes over you when you have to leave your child crying for you at daycare, with the babysitter or even their own dad. Their tears prick your heart and the guilt comes rushing in.

Or maybe it floods over you when you feel you have been too harsh or demanding—when it seems the only thing you've been doing all day long is yelling at your kids and doling out necessary discipline.

Guilt can drown us if we have been through a divorce, infidelity, or any shameful sin that reminds us of our failings. Every one of us carries guilt, maybe even when we shouldn't. But, how can we prevent it from controlling us?

Here's something to remember and distinguish: guilt combined with condemning thoughts is never from God. Guilt that leaves us with dark, self-deprecating thoughts and dwelling on what a bad person we are is a lie from the enemy. That kind of guilt causes us to carry a heavy load, one we were never intended to carry. It also prevents us from being the best parent we can be.

However, guilt that leads to repentance and a changed heart **is** from Him. The Bible calls it conviction. It's a tender pressing from the Holy Spirit that leans on our hearts, telling us that we have missed the mark of Love or are straying from His way.

This guilt is removed by the power of the risen Christ —an exchange that sets us free! Our shame has been nailed to the cross forever! It no longer exists, except in our own minds when the enemy pushes our buttons.

Our enemy wants us to believe we are bad moms and holds us hostage to our own convoluted thoughts. The guilt from our enemy is removed by constantly rejecting his condemnation and his lies and replacing the lies with truth.

You want to have a clear conscience knowing you did all you could to be a good mom to your kids today, in spite of your failings. If conviction is lingering at the end of the day, ask Him to reveal any area where you may have missed the mark with your family. Ask His forgiveness, and ask for the grace to apologize to them and try again tomorrow.

If the pressing by the Holy Spirit continues, don't shove that nagging feeling down, but rather bring it into the light. Pray over it. Share it with Jesus and your husband, or if you are single, a trusted advisor.

A change in your normal parenting practices, in the way you do life, or in your thoughts may be just what you need to set your heart free.

God is near. Trust Him with all your guilt. Reject the condemnation and live in freedom from your enemy's accusations. Embrace the conviction, believing that everything from God's hand is good, as He is shaping you into the likeness of His Son.

Father, please reveal to me any guilt I need to release and reject. Thank You that I don't have to carry it. I lay the shame of past events and present failings at Your feet, and I release them knowing that while those were real events, they do not define who I am now through You. Help me be open to You and those who love me most about any changes that need to be made, whether my circumstances or my heart, in order to live in true freedom. I thank You that You are loving, kind, and patient with me—walking with me every step, today and always.

Scripture readings:

- Psalms 32:1-5
- Isaiah 43:16-19
- Isaiah 43:25
- Romans 8:1-2
- 2 Corinthians 7:9-10
- 2 Corinthians 3:17
- 2 Corinthians 5:21
- Hebrews 9:14

In your own words, write down the difference in guilt and conviction.

Are you free from guilt, or does it weigh you down? Explain in your journal.

What is the greatest guilt you carry? Name it. Tell the story of when you first felt this guilt, then pray for God's healing over this source of shame.

What else causes you guilt?

Seeing it written, I now bring it to You, laying it at Your feet, Jesus. I release it to You, knowing that if I continue to carry it, it means that Your death was for nothing. Instead, I choose to live in Your resurrection power and move forward in You! Remind me every time I try to pick it up again.

He has removed our sins as far from us
as the east is from the west.

Psalms 103:12

29

WHO IS IN CHARGE?

The four-year-old seated in the grocery cart was wailing at the top of his lungs as his mother wheeled through the big box store where I was shopping. She was oblivious to his cries, allowing him free reign with his rage. You could hear his screams throughout the entire store and I noticed the concerned and annoyed looks on the faces of other patrons. Who was in charge here—the mom or the child?

I know I was guilty many times of allowing my children to take the lead. Our kids call us "mean, strict or old-school" and shy away from our guidelines. We are worn down by the multitude of requests and debates, the arguing and badgering, and we give in.

We concede when they tell us something is too hard, believing the lie that things are too difficult for them or they don't understand. We are stooping to the maturity level of our child as they are making a power play and winning. We have yielded our leadership and our child is now in charge.

If you are a single mom or have been through any traumatic event with your children you bear even more of these guilty feelings. Guilt causes us to back down from our standards and not press through. It can even cause us to baby our older children, and continue doing things for them well after they should have taken the responsibility for themselves. When we parent without consistency and structure, we create insecure children who are stunted in their growth and development.

Why do we give in? Because it's easier than standing firm. Avoiding conflict relieves a bit of that mom guilt, at least temporarily. Maybe our child won't think we are so mean or old-fashioned. Maybe they will like us better.

I have news for you: **God made you the parent**. You are not subject to your children, nor are you supposed to be their friend. Parenting is God's line of authority, and when we allow our children to wear us down, to step over and beyond us, we are allowing an avenue of chaos, disobedience, and insecurity into their lives. If we don't stop surrendering our authority now, we will leave a legacy of confusion and distrust, and someday our kids will be adults who can't obey God or stay in a healthy relationship.

Structure in your child's life is good. God is a God of order, not chaos. If we allow our children to set the bar, they will never reach their God-given potential. If we will stand, unwavering, against the demands, jabs, and complaints of our kids, we will see our children rise to the standards we set.

The dictionary defines the word "mother" as one who brings up another. Bringing up! Giving rise to our children. We are charged with leading them to a higher way. *The* Way!

Don't be like a ship—tossed back and forth on waves of indecision. Set standards fitting to you and your family based on the Word of God. Be kind, but firm, unmoving, and lead your children to the high path, one that will produce loving, secure adults.

Father, I admit I am weary and easily worn down. Add to that the guilt of my failings, and the fact that I just don't know what to do in some situations, most days I'm just a mess. It's no wonder my kids are, too. I'm asking You to lead me to new thoughts and ideas—ways to guide my children with consistency in the standards You've given me. I pray that as I search Your Word for direction, as I walk by Your side, I will be a strong example of guidance and security to my children. Help me not to be swayed by the complaints and cries of my children, but to hold firm to what I know is true and right. Give me boldness to step into giving rise to my children, knowing that as I find my security in You, I will be more secure in my parenting.

Scripture readings:

- Deuteronomy 12:28
- Proverbs 6:20
- Habakkuk 3:19
- 1 Corinthians 14:33
- Galatians 6:7-10
- Ephesians 4:14-16
- Ephesians 6:1
- Hebrews 12:7-12

Do you consider the God-given line of authority to be a blessing in the lives of your children? Why or why not?

Name some situations in which you may have given your children too much power or authority over you.

What keeps you from stepping fully into the role of leadership in their lives?

When and why are you inconsistent?

What effects have you noticed in your children as a result of inconsistent parenting? Explain.

mother

verb

1

a: to give birth to

b: to give rise to; produce

2

to care for or protect like a mother

30

UNIQUE

We were meeting at her house that day, so I entered her address in my map app so I could drive right to it. Unfortunately, I'd drive where the blue dot told me to go and it would indicate I had passed her location. After driving back and forth a few times, I looked around and noticed the most unusual house on the entire block. Of course, it was hers!

She welcomed me through the gates and into the serenity of a beautiful Japanese garden. Together we passed through the massive front door into a warm, eclectic mix of modern and Asian beauty that perfectly exemplified the freedom and peace of my new friend's heart.

We had met for coffee a few weeks earlier. She was concerned for her teen children and asked for some feedback. Were her kids missing out on something important in life, she wondered? They'd been given so much and lived a very different existence than most of their friends. Even at young ages, they had traveled the world on mission trips with their parents. Their life was one of abundance and plenty, but you'd never know it by their behavior. I was able to assure my friend that I certainly saw nothing wrong with her kids. In fact, I saw remarkable uniqueness expressed by this family's freedom and joy. It all pointed to their love for the Provider, Jesus, and a deep love for other people. It was something to celebrate!

God made each of our families special. Ask yourself: what is the unique quality of my family? What sets us apart from others? Maybe an easier question is what makes us—"us"?

For my family, it was the sheer numbers—the many. Having nine immediate family members is not common in today's society. Add to that home births, home education and living in the country, and well...that's just not what most people would consider normal.

What makes your family special? Did you adopt or foster children? Does your husband often work out of town? Is he in the military? A pastor? Are you a single mom? Do you have a special-needs child or a live-in grandparent? Are you a two-child family? All boys? A blended family? Maybe these are the exact things that will help train up your children in the way they need to go.

When we celebrate our uniqueness, I believe we gain a sense of belonging to a greater purpose. Realizing that we don't need to be like "everyone else" and teaching this to our children can establish a deep identity within them—an identity that will launch them into their individual purposes as they leave our homes and begin their own lives.

Celebrate the power of your family's distinctiveness and you'll inspire your children to use that foundation for God's glory!

Father, I admit, I've bucked against this entire idea. I compare my family to my friends' and it seems like we are just failing or missing it somewhere. Maybe the thing I think is tearing us apart is actually what is knitting us together. May I find joy in our uniqueness as I teach my family to celebrate who we are and who we will become through You.

Consider reading these scriptures from The Message:

- Proverbs 22:6
- Jeremiah1:5
- Matthew 23:11-12
- Romans 12:4-6
- Galatians 5:1
- Galatians 5:25-26
- Ephesians 4:7
- 1 Peter 2:9-12

What qualities set your family apart from others? Are you able to celebrate them as a gift from God? Make a list in your journal.

How can you celebrate these unique qualities with your children so they will see them as blessings? Write down your ideas.

If your children are young and your family's identity is not yet evident, what qualities do you and your husband want to instill in your family?

Take some time, perhaps during a date night, to discuss this.

If you are single, what qualities are important to you to impart to your kids? How can you appreciate this season in your life right now?

If this was a difficult series of questions for you to answer, spend some time asking God to reveal your family's distinct qualities. He will!

We will not hide these truths from our children; we will tell the next generation about the glorious deeds of the Lord, about his power and his mighty wonders.

Psalms 78:4

When I am...

Comparing myself to others: 23, 27

Depressed: 3, 7, 9, 11, 13, 17, 21

Discouraged: 4, 7, 9, 11, 17, 21, 22, 23, 24, 25

Dreading the day: 11

Emotional: 10, 11, 27

Fearful: 7, 9, 11, 13, 14, 17

Feeling the enemy: 6

Feeling guilt: 28, 29

Feeling pressured: 18, 19

Feeling unimportant: 5, 10, 21, 22, 30

Fighting negative thoughts: 9, 21, 25, 27

Frustrated: 9, 13, 15, 16, 18, 19, 20, 26

Impatient: 8, 12, 14, 26

In need of grace: 4, 5

Lonely: 4, 22

Needing Rest: 8

Not connecting with my husband: 13, 14, 25

Not liking my kids' behavior: 2, 8, 12, 14, 15, 16, 20, 24, 29

Struggling with my day: 7, 9, 10, 15, 22

Struggling with my words: 13, 24, 25

Tired: 1, 3, 4, 5

Weary: 1, 3, 15

ABOUT THE AUTHOR

Robin Meadows is the wife of one and the mom of many. She has been married to her husband Dirk for 44 years and together they raised and home-educated their seven children on a wooded acreage in central Oklahoma. The best part? All nine of them lived to tell about it!

Volume 2 of "Overwhelmed By My Blessings" will be available in 2019. In the meantime, find other devotional plans by Robin Meadows on YouVersion, the free Bible app, or connect with her on Instagram: @manymeadows

I pray that from his glorious, unlimited resources he will empower you with inner strength through his Spirit. Then Christ will make his home in your hearts as you trust in him. Your roots will grow down into God's love and keep you strong.

Ephesians 3:16-17

NOTES

Made in the USA
Columbia, SC
06 July 2020

12435605R00065